MEGAN RAPINOE

SOCCER SUPERSTAR

BY ANTHONY K. HEWSON

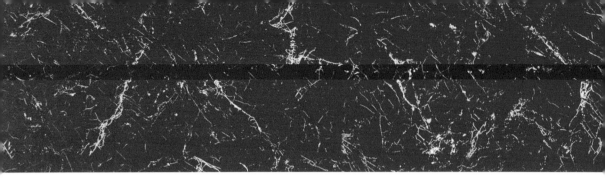

First Edition
First Printing, 2019

Book design by Jake Nordby
Cover design by Jake Nordby
Photographs ©: Christian Liewig/Abaca/Sipa USA/AP Images, cover, 1, 6, 25, back cover; Christophe Saidi/Sipa/AP Images, 4; DianeBentleyRaymond/iStockphoto, 8; Darren Abate/Getty Images Sport/Getty Images, 11; Jae C. Hong/AP Images, 13; Gregory Smith/AP Images, 14; Felice Calabró/AP Images, 17; EMPICS Sport/URN:14271181/Press Association/AP Images, 19; enterlinedesign/Shutterstock Images, 21; Petr David Josek/AP Images, 20; Jonathan Hayward/The Canadian Press/AP Images, 22; David Vincent/AP Images, 27; Jose Breton - Pics Action/Shutterstock Images, 30; Red Line Editorial, 29

Press Box Books, an imprint of Press Room Editions.

Library of Congress Control Number: 2019946260

ISBN
978-1-63494-201-0 (library bound)
978-1-63494-202-7 (paperback)
978-1-63494-203-4 (epub)
978-1-63494-204-1 (hosted ebook)

Distributed by North Star Editions, Inc.
2297 Waters Drive
Mendota Heights, MN 55120
www.northstareditions.com

Printed in the United States of America

About the Author

Anthony K. Hewson is a freelance writer. Originally from San Diego, he is now living in the Bay Area with his wife and their two dogs.

TABLE OF CONTENTS

1 CAPTAIN AMERICA

AUS player stood over the ball. Her light purple hair made it clear to the world it was Megan Rapinoe taking this free kick. And anyone who knew anything about soccer knew that could mean trouble for France.

In 2019 the US women's national team was going after a fourth Women's World Cup title. France, the tournament's host, stood in their way in the quarterfinals. In the game's fifth minute, Rapinoe had a chance to give her team a dream start.

Megan Rapinoe had the game of her life against France in the 2019 Women's World Cup.

Rapinoe strikes her iconic pose after scoring the first goal against France.

Rapinoe raised her left hand. She ran forward and booted a bending ball toward the goal. It zigzagged through a maze of legs toward the net. As if the ball had eyes, it avoided all obstructions and skipped into the back of the net.

The US players raced to celebrate with Rapinoe. But the star forward calmly walked to the sideline, outstretched her arms, and basked in the glory. It was just another outstanding moment for the US captain.

Later in the match, Rapinoe scored again to seal the US victory. But she also injured her leg. She finished the game, but she would have to miss the team's next match, a semifinal showdown with England. Rapinoe vowed that if her teammates won, she would be back for the final match of the tournament. She planned to finish the job.

COVER SHOT

Rapinoe's goal celebration against France became an iconic image from the Women's World Cup. It was shared all over social media and even ended up on the cover of *Sports Illustrated* magazine. Rapinoe said her celebration was meant to be fun and entertain the fans.

2 CLIMBING THE LADDER

Megan Rapinoe's first soccer idol was her older brother Brian. Megan had five siblings. But she wanted to be just like Brian. She played soccer because he played soccer. At their home in Redding, California, Brian taught her the game. He set up cones to run drills in the yard.

But Megan lost her role model when she was 10 years old. Brian was arrested for bringing drugs to school. He was 15. He became addicted to drugs and spent time in prison. Megan was heartbroken.

Megan grew up along the Sacramento River in the Northern California city of Redding.

Drug use was common where Megan grew up in Northern California. But Megan was able to avoid that trouble. She remained focused on soccer. Her first soccer coach was her dad. Jim Rapinoe coached her for most of her childhood until high school. Then Megan wanted tougher competition than what was available locally. She chose to play club soccer in Sacramento instead of playing for her high school team.

Club soccer did provide better competition. But Sacramento was a two-and-a-half-hour drive from Redding. The Rapinoes made the long round trip at least once during the week for practice and again

TWIN TEAMMATE

Megan has a twin sister named Rachael who also played soccer. The twins were teammates at the University of Portland. But Rachael's career was cut short by injuries. Rachael went on to start a soccer training company called Rapinoe SC. The sisters run the company together.

Megan and teammate Christine Sinclair helped Portland beat UCLA in the 2005 national championship game.

most weekends. The family went through three minivans during that time.

But the hard work and sacrifice paid off. Megan earned a scholarship to the University of Portland. And before her freshman season, she had another exciting opportunity. She played with the United States Women's National Team (USWNT) in the Under-19 Women's World Cup. She led the team with three goals in the tournament.

Megan didn't miss a beat when she got to Portland. As a freshman, she started all 25 games. She scored 15 goals and ended up with 13 assists. The Pilots went undefeated and won the national championship.

That summer, Megan got another chance with the national team. This time, it was the senior team. Megan played in a friendly against Ireland in July. She played another one against Taiwan in October and scored two goals.

But just eight days after the Taiwan match, Megan suffered her first serious injury—a torn knee ligament. She had to miss the rest of her sophomore season. The next year, she suffered

Megan made her debut with the USWNT in 2006.

the same injury two games into her junior season. Megan was almost totally out of action for two years. Once healthy, she decided to turn pro.

3 A RISING STAR

Megan Rapinoe was the first-ever draft pick of the Chicago Red Stars. The Red Stars played in Women's Professional Soccer (WPS), a new league that started in 2009. Rapinoe was the second overall pick.

Rapinoe was a WPS All-Star in Chicago. But the team and the league were on shaky financial ground. The Red Stars folded in 2010. Rapinoe then bounced around to a couple other WPS

Rapinoe, celebrating a goal against China in 2010, quickly became a leader on the USWNT.

teams and even played for a club in Australia. The WPS itself folded in 2012.

Still, Rapinoe was always on firm ground with the US national team. After missing 2007 and 2008 due to her knee injuries, Rapinoe burst back onto the scene in 2009. She started six matches and scored the lone goal in a 1–0 win against Norway.

The US women had been one of the best teams in the world for decades. But they weren't as dominant in 2010. The team lost to Mexico with a spot in the 2011 Women's World Cup on the line. That meant they had to play Italy twice to determine the final team to qualify.

The Americans won the first match 1–0 in Italy. Back home in the United States, Rapinoe helped clinch the second. Just before halftime she used her dribbling skills to cut into the

Rapinoe used her head to help the USWNT defeat Italy in 2010.

open field. She then hammered a shot at the keeper, who stopped it but couldn't control the ball. US teammate Amy Rodriguez was there to bury the rebound. The Americans held on for another 1–0 victory.

At the Women's World Cup, Rapinoe showed off more of her skills. The Americans were on the verge of elimination in the quarterfinals. The match had gone to extra time, and Brazil was up 2–1.

In the 122nd minute, the US team was scrambling for one last chance. Rapinoe had the ball on the left sideline when she saw an opening. She delivered a 45-yard (40-m) crossing pass. It veered across the field, where it met up with Abby Wambach's forehead. The US star headed it past Brazil's keeper. The US then won in a penalty shootout.

Rapinoe and her teammates came through against Japan in the 2012 Olympic final.

It looked like the US women were on their way to another title. But they were shocked by Japan in a shootout in the final. Redemption came in London the next summer, when they beat Japan 2–1 to win the Olympic gold medal. Rapinoe scored three goals in the tournament, including two in a tense semifinal win over Canada. Rapinoe came up big when her team needed her most.

THE CROSS

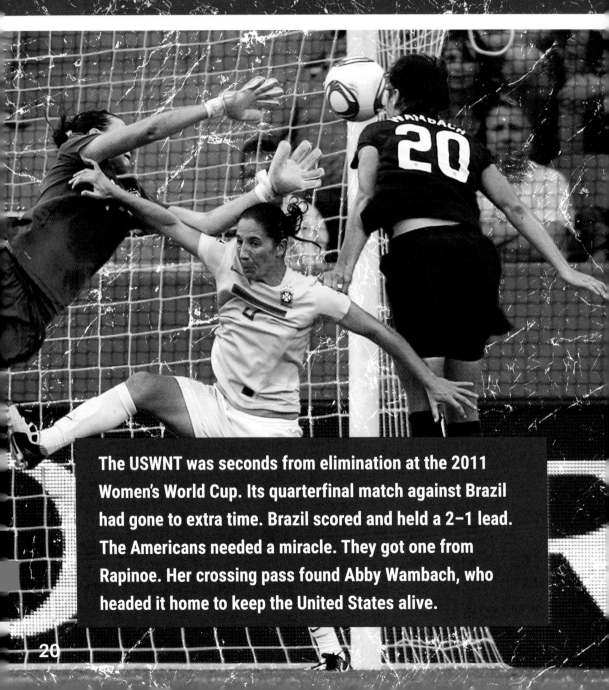

The USWNT was seconds from elimination at the 2011 Women's World Cup. Its quarterfinal match against Brazil had gone to extra time. Brazil scored and held a 2–1 lead. The Americans needed a miracle. They got one from Rapinoe. Her crossing pass found Abby Wambach, who headed it home to keep the United States alive.

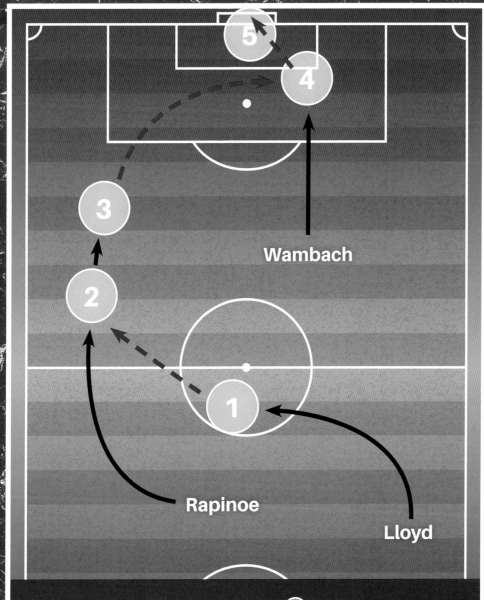

5

4

3

Wambach

2

1

Rapinoe

Lloyd

The ball started with Carli Lloyd, who ① passed to Rapinoe on the left flank ②. Rapinoe took one dribble and sent a long cross ③ to Wambach, who was calling for the ball in the box. Wambach leapt high and headed the ball ④ past Brazil's keeper and into the back of the net ⑤. The goal sent the match to a penalty shootout, which the United States won.

4 LEADING THE WAY

After spending time playing for a club in France, Rapinoe found a pro soccer home. In 2013 she signed with Seattle Reign FC in the new National Women's Soccer League (NWSL). The team was 0-9-1 when she joined them. But with Rapinoe's help, they turned their season around. She led the team in goals despite playing in only 12 of 22 games. Rapinoe had finally found a professional home.

Rapinoe and her teammates had plenty to celebrate during the 2015 Women's World Cup.

At the same time, Rapinoe helped the United States qualify for the 2015 Women's World Cup in Canada. After their loss in 2011, the Americans had unfinished business. The USWNT faced Australia in its first match in Winnipeg, Manitoba, and Rapinoe came ready to play. In the 12th minute, she gained control of a loose ball. She had three defenders in front of her at the top of the box. Rapinoe fired a shot that deflected off one of them and spun past the goalkeeper.

She wasn't done scoring. In the second half, Rapinoe gathered the ball at midfield and dribbled deep into Australia territory. Then she cut around a defender in the box and hit a perfectly placed shot into the far corner of the net. The Americans won 3–1 and went on to win the Women's World Cup.

Rapinoe showed no signs of slowing down in the 2019 Women's World Cup.

Even as Rapinoe entered her 30s, she continued to play with the fire of a champion. By 2019, she was co-captain of the national team. And she and her teammates were eager to become the first US squad to win consecutive Women's World Cup titles.

Rapinoe had the tournament of her career. She scored twice on penalty kicks as the Americans beat Spain 2–1. Then they faced France in the quarterfinals. Rapinoe opened the scoring on a free kick. In the second half, US winger Tobin Heath crossed the ball toward the top of the box. Rapinoe was waiting there. She hammered it home, and the United States again won 2–1.

An injury kept Rapinoe out of the semifinal match against England, but her teammates came through and she was back for the final against the Netherlands. After a

ACTIVISM

Rapinoe has spent much of her time off the soccer field advocating for equal rights, both for gay people like herself and for others in minority groups. She also has made on-field protests to bring attention to important issues. Sometimes her views have been controversial. But Rapinoe is not one to back down. To her, being an American means standing up for what you believe in.

Rapinoe got the United States on the board with a successful penalty kick against the Netherlands.

scoreless first half, US striker Alex Morgan was fouled in the box. It was Rapinoe's time to step up again. She converted the penalty kick for a 1–0 US lead. The United States held on to win the Women's World Cup. Rapinoe tied Morgan for the tournament lead in goals. She won the Golden Ball as the tournament's best player. Rapinoe proved she was still one of the best players in the world.

TIMELINE

1. **Redding, California (July 5, 1985)**
   Megan Rapinoe is born.

2. **Portland, Oregon (2005)**
   Rapinoe begins her college soccer career at the University of Portland.

3. **San Diego, California (July 23, 2006)**
   Rapinoe makes her senior national team debut in a friendly against Ireland.

4. **Carson, California (October 1, 2006)**
   Rapinoe scores her first goal for the United States against Taiwan.

5. **Sinsheim, Germany (July 2, 2011)**
   Rapinoe scores her first Women's World Cup goal against Colombia.

6. **Winnipeg, Manitoba, Canada (June 8, 2015)**
   Rapinoe scores two goals in the US Women's World Cup opener against Australia.

7. **Lyon, France (July 7, 2019)**
   Rapinoe wins her second World Cup with the US national team in a 2-0 victory over the Netherlands and picks up two individual trophies—the Golden Boot as the tournament's leading scorer and the Golden Ball as the tournament's top player.

MAP

Birth date: July 5, 1985

Birthplace:
Redding, California

Position: Forward

Height: 5 feet 7 inches

Current team: Reign FC
(2013–) and United States
women's national team
(2006–)

Previous teams: University
of Portland (2005–08),
Chicago Red Stars (2009–10),
Philadelphia Independence
(2011), magicJack (2011),
Sydney FC (2011), Seattle Sounders Women (2012), Olympique
Lyonnais (2013–14)

Major awards: Women's World Cup Golden Ball (2019), Women's
World Cup Golden Boot (2019), Women's World Cup champion
(2015, 2019), Olympic gold medalist (2012)

Accurate through the 2019 Women's World Cup.

GLOSSARY

advocate
To publicly support a particular cause.

cross
A pass delivered from the side of the field toward the middle.

draft
An event that allows teams to choose new players coming into the league.

extra time
An overtime period in soccer played when regulation time ends in a tie.

free kick
A kick from a set distance with no interference from the defense.

friendly
A match that soccer teams play that is not part of any official competition.

ligament
Tissue that connects bones with each other.

scholarship
Money given to a student to pay for educational expenses, sometimes in exchange for playing sports.

vow
To promise.

TO LEARN MORE

Books

Carothers, Thomas. *Women's World Cup Heroes*. Minneapolis: Abdo Publishing, 2019.

Marthaler, Jon. *US Women's Professional Soccer*. Minneapolis: Abdo Publishing, 2019.

Terrell, Brandon. *Soccer Showdown: U.S. Women's Stunning 1999 World Cup Win*. North Mankato, MN: Capstone, 2019.

Websites

NWSL Bio
http://www.nwslsoccer.com/players/megan-rapinoe

Rapinoe SC Official Website
http://www.rapinoe.us

US Soccer Bio
https://www.ussoccer.com/players/r/megan-rapinoe

INDEX